Jordy's Pets

Jordy likes reptiles even though most people don't. Jordy has a pet snake and a pet lizard at home. Her dad never comes into her room when her pets are out, but Jordy and her mom play with them all the time. Jordy hopes to get a turtle for her birthday.

Circle the correct detail in each sentence.

1. Jordy (likes, dislikes) reptiles.

2. A snake (is, is not) a reptile.

3. Jordy's mother (likes, dislikes) reptiles.

4. Jordy (wants, does not want) a turtle.

5. Jordy's father (likes, dislikes) snakes.

Circle yes or no.

6. Jordy wants a pet rat.   yes   no

7. A lizard is a reptile.   yes   no

8. Most people like reptiles.   yes   no

Reading Can Be Painful

One afternoon I was sitting under a tree reading a book when suddenly I felt something hit the top of my head. I reached up to see what it was. I felt something small, smooth, and hard. It was an acorn. Just then I heard a squirrel scamper away. I think he was laughing at me.

Answer the questions.

1. What do you think happened next? _____

_____

2. Why do you think that? _____

_____

3. What do you think the author will do the next time before she sits down under a tree to read?

_____

_____

In the space below, draw a picture of what the character's face looked like as the squirrel scampered away.

A Dinosaur Named Sue

   In Chicago, there is a dinosaur named Sue. Sue is a Tyranno-saurus rex. She is the largest and most complete T. rex ever found. Her skeleton is on display at the Field Museum. She waited 67 million years to be found. A fossil hunter named Sue Hendrickson uncovered her. That's how she got her name.

Follow the directions.

1. Circle the main idea of the story.

   There is a T. rex in Chicago named Sue.

   Dinosaur fossils are hard to find.

   Sue Hendrickson is a fossil hunter.

2. Underline the true statements.

   Sue was named for the person who discovered her.

   It's easy to find complete dinosaur skeletons.

   Sue is on display at the Field Museum.

4

Use the Word List to find the words related to dinosaurs in the word search.

Word List
claws
dinosaur
extinct
fossil
hunter
jaws
skeleton

```
        x
    q e u
    q p n q t
    j a w s t u d
  d m z q e t f i
s k x c l a w s n
d k x t u o x l o
k e e n o y r v s
q x f l p b p r a q
x t h o e h e h u m c
q i z e s t n o r k h
k n b g n s o u o k q o
c u u a o i n d v o b
t h r a s n l q y c h
```

My Backyard Bunny

Mr. Wiggins is a rabbit that lives in my backyard. He likes to hide in the bushes. He also hides behind the flowerpots. He pretends that he is wild and eats the grass, but he likes the vegetables and fruits we leave out for him better. He even likes to eat crackers and cereal. Sometimes he lets me rub his head. He's not really wild.

Answer the questions.

1. What is the name of the rabbit? _____

_____

2. Where does the rabbit like to hide? _____

_____

6

3. What does the rabbit eat? _____

_____

4. Why do you think the author says this rabbit isn't really wild?

_____

5. Do you think the author lives in a house or an apartment? How can you tell?

_____

_____

6. Does the author like the rabbit? How do you know?

_____

_____

7. Do you think this rabbit would be a good pet? Why?

_____

_____

Early Humans

How is it possible to learn about the lives of **prehistoric** people? Luckily, early humans left behind some **remains** of their daily lives. Objects they made and used became covered over by earth long ago. **Archaeologists** dig up these remains and try to figure out what they mean. One thing they have learned is that human beings are the only animals who are able to **manufacture** tools and pass this **knowledge** on to others.

Draw a line to match each word to its definition.

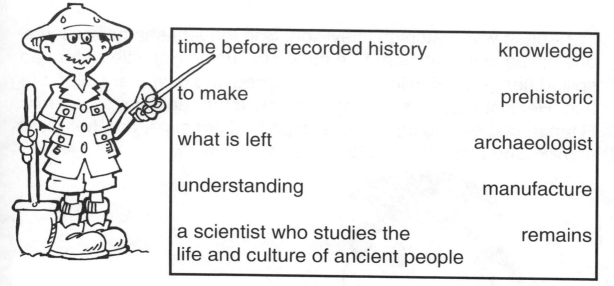

time before recorded history	knowledge
to make	prehistoric
what is left	archaeologist
understanding	manufacture
a scientist who studies the life and culture of ancient people	remains

Answer the questions.

1. How can we learn about prehistoric people? _____

_____

2. Why do you think the author says that people are lucky to find the buried objects of prehistoric people?

_____

_____

3. According to the passage, what can humans do that other animals cannot?

_____

_____

Spilled Milk

Hannah was watching television. She thought she heard someone crying in the kitchen. She got up to check. Her little sister had spilled her glass of milk. Hannah laughed and gave her sister a big hug. Her sister stopped crying and asked for another glass of milk. Hannah cleaned up the mess and poured her sister another glass of milk. She then returned to her television show.

Answer the questions.

1. What caused Hannah to leave her television program and go to the kitchen?

   _____

2. What effect did hugging her sister have? _____

   _____

3. What caused Hannah to pour her sister another glass of milk?

   _____

4. What effect do you think this accident had on the way her sister will drink the next glass of milk?

   _____

Write a paragraph about a time when you spilled something. What caused the spill, and what effect did it have on you?

_____

_____

_____

_____

_____

A Walk around the Block

Cali went for a walk around the neighborhood with her uncle. She stopped and pointed at many things she saw along the way.

She saw an ant carry a tiny leaf across the sidewalk. She saw a bird on a tree branch. She saw an odd-shaped rock stuck in the mud.

When they got back home, her uncle laughed and said, "That wasn't much of a walk; it was more like a look!"

Number the events in the correct order.

_____ Cali saw a rock in the mud.

_____ Cali saw a bird in a tree.

_____ Cali and her uncle went for a walk.

_____ Cali's uncle made a joke.

_____ Cali watched an ant carry a leaf.

Circle the **best** answer to complete the sentence.

When Cali's uncle takes her for a walk around the neighborhood again, her uncle will probably…

plan more time for the walk.

bring bird seed on the walk.

get a new pair of walking shoes.

In the space below, draw a picture of something Cali might see on her next walk around the block.

Bill Pickett

Bill Pickett was a **tough** cowboy. He was born in 1870 and is called the father of **steer wrestling**. He was not a big man. Bill only weighed 145 pounds, but he could bring down a 1,000-pound steer with no **difficulty**. How did he do it? He bit the steer on its **slobbery** bottom lip. He learned that **technique** by watching dogs work the herds. Bill died in 1932 along with his wrestling style. Nobody bites steers during rodeo **events** today.

Circle the correct answer.

1. Bill Pickett was a(n)

   clown.　cowboy.　astronaut.

2. He was born in

   1870.　1963.　2003.

3. Bill weighed 145

   tons.　ounces.　pounds.

4. He bit the steer on its

   ear.　foot.　lip.

5. He learned the technique watching

   dogs.　horses.　pigs.

14

Write the words from Pickett's lasso next to the correct meanings.

difficulty   steer
event   technique
herd   tough
slobbery   wrestling

strong _____

a sport _____

unpleasantly wet, slimy _____

a way of doing something _____

a happening _____

trouble _____

cow _____

a group of cattle_____

Cat Rescuer

My aunt is a cat rescuer. She saves injured stray cats, and rescues pet cats that have been abandoned at the animal shelter. I asked her to come to my class and tell us about her job. She came and talked about what her job was like. The class enjoyed her visit. She showed us pictures of the cats she has rescued. She even brought her favorite cat. When she was done, the class clapped for a long time. I was very proud of my aunt.

Follow the directions.

1. Circle the sentence that tells the main idea.
2. With a red crayon, draw a line under the sentence that tells the most about the aunt's job.
3. With a blue crayon, draw a line under the sentence that tells how the author felt about her aunt.

Use the words in the box to help you complete the summary.

abandoned	clapped	job	rescuer
aunt	favorite	pictures	rescues
cats	injured	proud	saves

My aunt came to my class to tell us about her job. She _____

_____

_____

_____

I was proud of her because _____

_____

_____

_____

Cockroaches

Cockroaches have been on earth for thousands of years. They were here before the dinosaurs. They have hard shells that act like armor. They have good hearing and eyesight. They give birth to as many as 30,000 baby cockroaches every year. Cockroaches eat almost anything but can go three months without food. They can even go 30 days without water. Cockroaches don't bite or hurt humans. So why do people scream and run when they see them?

Read each sentence. Circle F if the sentence is a fact or O if the sentence is an opinion.

	Fact	Opinion
1. Cockroaches have hard shells.	F	O
2. Cockroaches have good eyesight.	F	O
3. Cockroaches are ugly.	F	O
4. Cockroaches eat almost anything.	F	O
5. Cockroaches don't bite humans.	F	O

List one detail in each oval to complete the story web. The main idea and one detail are done for you.

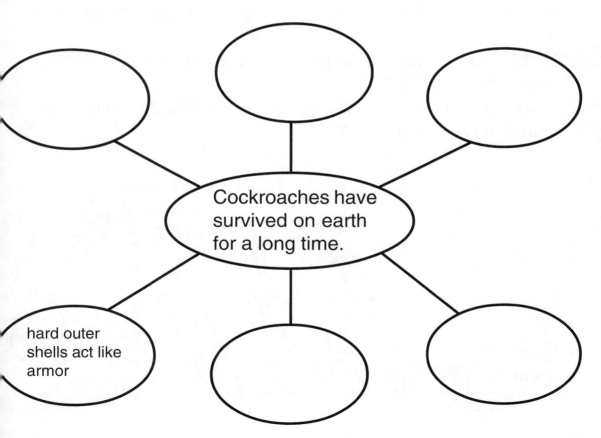

Going Fishing!

Dan was still excited when he went to bed. He and his dad had had a big day. First, they went out to breakfast and ordered pancakes. Next, they went to a big store. Dan and his dad bought some fishing line, sinkers, and hooks. They also got Dan a new rod and reel. Then, the two went shopping for some clothes. They got a pair of shorts for Dad, a T-shirt for each of them, and a new cap for Dan. Finally, Dan and his dad hunted for worms. Dan and his dad were getting ready to go fishing.

Follow the directions.

1. With a red crayon, underline the sentence that tells what Dan and his dad did first.
2. With a blue crayon, underline the sentence that tells what happened next.
3. With a green crayon, underline the sentence that tells what Dan and his dad finally did.

Answer the questions.

4. The main idea of this story is that Dan _____

_____

5. List three places Dan and his dad went. _____

_____

_____

6. List five things Dan and his dad bought. _____

_____

_____

7. Do you think Dan was excited about the trip? Why? _____

_____

_____

In the space below, draw a picture of what else you would want to take on a fishing trip.

Together Again

Oscar and Clarice were brother and sister. They lived together in the same cage at the animal shelter. Oscar was a big, loud kitten. Clarice was tiny and shy. One day, Tom and his father came into the animal shelter to pick out a kitten. Tom liked Oscar but his father thought Clarice would make a better pet. They brought Clarice home but she was not happy. She hid behind everything, meowed all night, and wouldn't eat. The next day Tom and his dad went back to the shelter. They decided to adopt Oscar, too.

Answer the questions.

1. If Tom liked Oscar, what caused him to pick Clarice?

_____

_____

22

2. What was the effect of Clarice's separation from Oscar?

_____

_____

3. What caused Tom and his dad to go back to the shelter to get Oscar?

_____

_____

4. What do you think will be the effect of Tom bringing Oscar home?

_____

_____

Write another paragraph to finish this story.

_____

_____

_____

_____

_____

Fan Tan

"Fan Tan" is a number game that started in China. This fun math game is a variation of "Fan Tan" that you can play, too.

To start, make a simple game board from a plain piece of paper. Number the corners 0 through 3 (one number per corner). Each player should pick a number between 0 and 3 and write his or her name next to that number on the paper. One player should take a handful of beans and place it on the paper. The beans should be counted out into four equal piles. The game is over when there are no beans left to distribute equally. The person whose number matches the number of beans remaining is the winner.

Number the steps to play "Fan Tan" in order from 1 to 7.

_____ Number the corners 0 through 3.

_____ Count out the beans in four equal piles.

_____ Make a game board.

_____ The winner is the person whose number matches the number of beans remaining.

_____ Write your name next to the number you pick.

_____ Pick a number between 0 and 3.

_____ Take a handful of beans and place it in the middle of the game board.

Write a paragraph explaining how to play your favorite game.

_____

_____

_____

_____

_____

_____

First-Time Skater

Tina went skating for the first time on Saturday. She was really scared and held on tightly to her friend's hand. Tina was afraid she would fall, and she did fall a few times. She skated around the skating rink, then stopped to rest. She did this for more than an hour, then it was time to go.

Tina quickly took off her skates and put them on the counter. Her friend felt bad and thought Tina didn't have a good time. She asked Tina if she wanted to go skating again sometime. Her friend was surprised when Tina said with a great big smile, "How about tomorrow?"

Use the information in the story to complete the summary.

The main character is _____ . She was going

_____ with her friend. She was afraid

because_____

_____. Her friend helped

her by _____.

Tina and her friend planned to _____

_____.

Use details from the story to answer the following question.

Why do you think Tina's friend was surprised when Tina told her she wanted to go skating again?

_____

_____

_____

_____

Read the statements and follow the directions at the top of the next page **before** you read the passage.

Hamsters

Hamsters are wild in some parts of the world, but can make good pets. Hamsters are fun to watch and easy to handle. Hamsters are related to mice and rats. They all belong to an animal family called rodents. Rodents have front teeth that continue to grow all through their life. They gnaw on things to stop their front teeth from getting too long. Hamsters are nocturnal. This means that they sleep in the day and stay up at night. Hamsters have poor eyesight. If you stood more than about five steps away from one, it probably would not see you. Hamsters have very good hearing and do not like sudden or loud noises. Hamsters recognize things by how they smell rather than how they look.

Read each statement. Check the set of boxes on the left to indicate whether you think the statements are true or false. **After** reading the passage, check the set of boxes on the right to see if you still feel the same way about each statement.

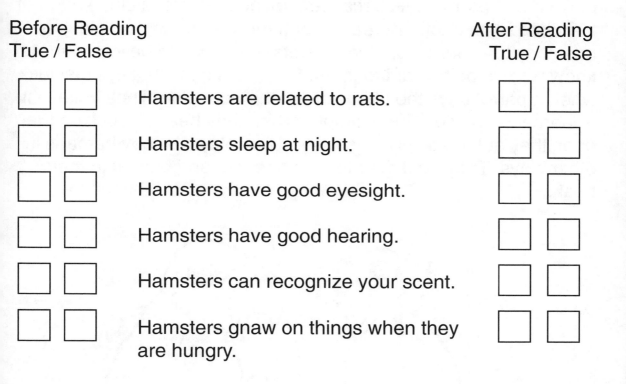

Before Reading
True / False

After Reading
True / False

Hamsters are related to rats.

Hamsters sleep at night.

Hamsters have good eyesight.

Hamsters have good hearing.

Hamsters can recognize your scent.

Hamsters gnaw on things when they are hungry.

If you had a hamster, what could be some problems you might have keeping it as a pet?

_____

_____

_____

_____

Parrots

I love to listen to parrots talk. They can copy the sounds that people make, but nobody knows how they do it. Some scientists believe that parrots talk because they need to feel a close bond or friendship with another creature or their owners. In the wild, parrots copy the sounds of other parrots. Bird owners believe parrots know what is being said to them. Scientists think that it is just luck when a parrot says the right word at the right time. They believe it is learned behavior. For example, when they hear a knock on the door, they automatically say, "Hello." Parrots also copy humans in other ways. They hold their food in one foot and bring it to their beak.

Reading Comprehension: Grade 3 Answer Key

Page 1
1. likes
2. is
3. likes
4. wants
5. dislikes
6. no
7. yes
8. no

Page 3
Answers and pictures will vary.

Page 4
1. There is a T. rex in Chicago named Sue.
2. Sue was named for the person who discovered her.
   Sue is on display at the Field Museum.

Page 5

Page 6
1. The name of the rabbit is Mr. Wiggins.
2. The rabbit likes to hide in the bushes and behind the flowerpots.

Page 7
3. He eats grass, vegetables and fruits, crackers, and cereal.
4. He lets the author rub his head.
5. The author probably lives in a house because he has a backyard.
6. The author likes the rabbit because he feeds him and rubs his head.
7. Answers will vary.

Page 9

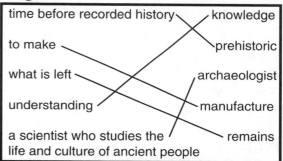

1. We can learn about prehistoric people by studying the remains of their daily lives.
2. Answers will vary.
3. Humans can manufacture tools and pass along this knowledge.

Page 11
1. She heard someone crying.
2. Her sister stopped crying.
3. She asked for another glass of milk.
4. She will be more careful next time.
Paragraphs will vary.

Page 12
 4 Cali saw a rock in the mud.
 3 Cali saw a bird in the tree.
 1 Cali and her uncle went for a walk.
 5 Cali's uncle made a joke.
 2 Cali watched an ant carry a leaf.

A

Page 13
"Plan more time for the walk" should be circled.
Pictures will vary.

Page 14
1. cowboy.
2. 1870.
3. pounds.
4. lip.
5. dogs.

Page 15
strong: tough
a sport: wrestling
unpleasantly wet, slimy: slobbery
a way of doing something: technique
a happening: event
trouble: difficulty
cow: steer
a number of cattle: herd

Page 16
1. Circle: My aunt is a cat rescuer.
2. Red line: She saves injured stray cats and rescues pet cats that have been abandoned at the animal shelter.
3. Blue line: I was very proud of my aunt.

Page 17
Answers will vary.

Page 19
1. F
2. F
3. O
4. F
5. F

Details can include:
   were here before dinosaurs
   have good hearing
   have good eyesight
   can go 30 days without water
   eat almost anything
   can go three months without food
   give birth to up to 30,000 babies/year

Page 20
1. Red line: First, they went out to breakfast and ordered pancakes.
2. Blue line: Next, they went to a big store.
3. Green line: Finally, Dan and his dad hunted for worms.

Page 21
4. Dan and his dad were getting ready to go fishing.
5. Answer should include three of the following: to breakfast, to a big store, clothes shopping, and hunting for worms.
6. Answer should include five of the following: fishing line, sinkers, hooks, new rod and reel, shorts, T-shirts, and cap.
7. Answers will vary.
Pictures will vary.

Page 22
1. His dad thought Clarice would make a better pet.

Page 23
2. Clarice hid, meowed all night, and wouldn't eat.
3. Clarice was unhappy without Oscar.
4. Answers will vary.
Paragraphs will vary.

Page 25
2 Number the corners 0 through 3.
6 Count out the beans in four equal...
1 Make a game board.
7 The winner is the person whose...
4 Write your name next to the...
3 Pick a number between 0 and 3.
5 Take a handful of beans and ...
Paragraphs will vary.

B

Page 27

The main character is <u>Tina</u>. She was going <u>skating</u> with her friend. She was afraid because <u>she thought she would fall</u>. Her friend helped her by <u>holding on to her tightly</u>. Tina and her friend planned to <u>skate again tomorrow</u>. Answers will vary.

Page 29

Hamsters are related to rats.	T
Hamsters sleep at night.	F
Hamsters have good eyesight.	F
Hamsters have good hearing.	T
Hamsters can recognize your scent.	T
Hamsters gnaw on things when...	F

Answers will vary.

Page 31

1. parrots
2. talk
3. scientists
4. owners
5. know
6. saying
7. learned
8. copy

Page 33

SD	Dardan is from Kosovo.
M	Dardan can't figure out why...
SD	Dardan learned how to speak...
SD	Dardan is very tall for his age.
SD	Dardan is 14 years old.
SD	Dardan likes to play soccer.

Answers will vary.

Page 35

1. True
2. False
3. False
4. True
5. True
6. True
7. True
8. False

As a fish lets water in its mouth, the water flows over the gills and the fish's body takes the oxygen it needs.

Page 37

8 The games ends when everyone...
3 Put the scarf in the center of the...
1 Choose one player to be It.
2 Form a circle around It.
6 Grab the scarf and run to an empty...
4 Pick a player to be the Thief who...
5 Both players try to grab the scarf.
7 The person that gets tagged...
Answers will vary.

Page 39

1. celebrate her birthday.
2. She almost fainted.
3. She looked tired.
4. They didn't have much money, and they knew Marcia would like it.
5. Answers can include: made waffles, went on a picnic, let her nap, made dinner, did laundry, cleaned the house, and put on a skit.
6. Answers will vary.

Page 41

1. Answers will vary. (He had a bad day.)
2. Answer should include three details from the story.
3. Answers will vary.
4. Answers will vary.
5. Answers will vary.

Page 43

1. Earthquakes
2. Titles will vary.
3. Earthquakes are scary natural disasters.
4. Answers will vary.

Earthquakes are — scary natural disasters.
Fires occur... — from broken water pipes.
Flood happen — gas pipes break.
The main shock — is the strongest part...
Aftershocks — are smaller quakes.
An earthquake... — with foreshocks.

Page 45

<u>5</u> Let somebody else have a turn...
<u>1</u> Make a beanbag or sock filled with...
<u>2</u> Decorate the beanbag with feathers.
<u>4</u> Say a letter or count while you are...
<u>3</u> Take turns tossing the bag up and...
Answers will vary.

Page 47

Main Character: Ben
Setting: Park
Plot: Ben found a leprechaun in the park. He thought about things to wish for. He wished for a hot fudge sundae. He dripped chocolate on his shirt. His mother grounded him for one week.
Answers will vary.

Page 49

Answers and pictures will vary.

Page 51

1. d
2. c
3. b
4. a
5. e
Paragraphs will vary.

Page 53

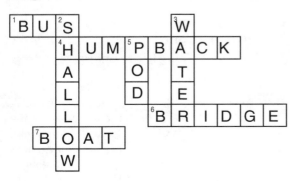

Page 55

1. a
2. c
3. b
4. a
5. kept the pebble from bouncing at all.
6. Answers will vary.

Page 57

1. They set up the tent and got out the supplies for dinner.
2. He went exploring and found a snake.
3. He ran back to camp, jumped into the car, and closed the door.
4. Answers will vary.

Page 59

1. meet
2. eternity
3. sobbed
4. train
5. competition
6. announced
7. embarrassed
8. stubborn

Page 60

1. a pet
2. The author's mom thinks he should think about his choice because it is a big responsibility and he can only choose once.
3. Answers should include three of the following: puppy, guppies, cat, lizard, frog, and rat.
4. Answers will vary.

D

Use the words in the box to complete the summary. Write your answers on the lines.

copy	learned	Parrots	scientists
know	owners	saying	talk

_____ (1) are interesting birds. They can _____ (2) but

_____ (3) don't know why or how. Bird_____ (4) believe

their birds _____ (5) what they are _____ (6). Scientists

believe it is just _____ (7) behavior. Parrots seem to like to

_____ (8) people.

1. _____

2. _____

3. _____

4. _____

5. _____

6. _____

7. _____

8. _____

An American Custom?

Dardan was new to the United States. He and his family moved here from Kosovo, a region of the European country Yugoslavia. So far he really liked his new country. He learned English quickly and made lots of friends. He studied hard and made very good grades in school.

There was just one thing that puzzled him. Everyone he met said, "You must be a great basketball player." Dardan was tall, very tall for someone just 14 years old, but he didn't care that much about basketball. He actually liked soccer better. So why did everyone want to push him to be a basketball player? The only thing he could figure out was that if you are a tall American you must need to play basketball to make everyone happy. What a strange custom!

Write an M next to the sentence that states the main idea of the story.
Write an SD next to the sentences that are supporting details in the story.

_____ Dardan is from Kosovo.

_____ Dardan can't figure out why everybody expects him to be a
basketball player.

_____ Dardan learned how to speak English and does very well in
school.

_____ Dardan is very tall for his age.

_____ Dardan is 14 years old.

_____ Dardan likes to play soccer.

If you were to answer Dardan's question, what would you say?

_____

_____

_____

_____

_____

_____

_____

Fish

Fish are made just right for living underwater. They have sleek bodies that are perfect for swimming. They also have fins that help them move. Their tail fins push them through the water. The other fins help them steer or stop.

Most fish have skin that is covered with scales. These hard, clear scales help the fish swim, too. Scales help the fish slide easily through the water.

Fish have gills for breathing. A fish opens its mouth and lets water in. When the fish closes its mouth, the water flows over the gills inside its body. A fish's body takes the oxygen it needs from the water.

Fish are cold-blooded. This means that their body temperature matches the temperature of the water around them. Fish don't have eyelids and can't cry, so the water keeps their eyes washed. The underwater world is perfect for fish.

Read each statement about fish. Decide if the statement is true or false and circle the appropriate word.

1. Most fish have scales.   True   False

2. Fish have lungs.   True   False

3. Fish are warm-blooded.   True   False

4. Fish don't have eyelids.   True   False

5. Tail fins push fish through the water.   True   False

6. Fins help a fish steer.   True   False

7. Fish have sleek bodies.   True   False

8. Fish can cry.   True   False

Explain how a fish breathes.

_____

_____

_____

_____

Jenny's Game

One day, Jenny decided to teach her friends how to play a game that she learned at camp. To play the game, she chose one player to be "It," and had her friends make a big circle around that player. Then, she tied a scarf in a knot and placed it on the ground in the middle of the circle. Next, she asked the player who was "It" to pick a player to be the "Thief" and move into the circle with "It." She told both players to try and grab the scarf. The player who grabbed the scarf had to run to the empty spot on the circle left by the "Thief" without being tagged by the other player. The person who got tagged became "It" for the next round. The game ended when everyone had a turn.

Number the steps to play Jenny's game in order from 1 to 8.

_____ The game ends when everyone has had a turn.

_____ Put the scarf in the center of the circle.

_____ Choose one player to be "It."

_____ Form a circle around "It."

_____ Grab the scarf and run to an empty spot in the circle.

_____ Pick a player to be the "Thief" who goes in the circle with "It."

_____ Both players try to grab the scarf.

_____ The person that gets tagged becomes "It" for the next round.

What would you do to make this game more fun or a little more difficult?

_____

_____

_____

_____

_____

Marcia's Big Day

Marcia's family wanted her 40th birthday to be her best birthday ever, but they didn't have much money. So they made her home-made waffles for breakfast. For lunch, they took a picnic to the ballpark because Marcia loves playing softball. They brought to-mato sandwiches and fresh fruit because they knew Marcia would like them.

When they went home, they thought Marcia looked tired, so they put a pillow under her head and let her take a nap. Then, Marcia's family made dinner, did the laundry, and cleaned the house. Marcia almost fainted.

After dinner, they washed the dishes and put them away. Marcia thanked them, but that wasn't all! Her son and daughter asked her to sit on the living room couch while they put on a skit. Marcia laughed and laughed and said that this was her best birthday ever!

Answer the questions.

1. Marcia's family planned a special day to _____

   _____

2. What did Marcia do when her family made dinner, did the
   laundry, and cleaned the house?

   _____

3. Why did her family let Marcia take a nap? _____

   _____

4. Why did Marcia's family go on a picnic instead of to a restaurant?

   _____

   _____

5. List some of the things her family did because they wanted to
   make Marcia happy.

   _____

   _____

6. How would you like to spend your perfect birthday? _____

   _____

   _____

Luis's Terrible Day

Luis was having a terrible day. He woke up late for school, and then had to rush through breakfast. He only got one bite of toast before the bus arrived. On his way to the bus, he dropped his homework in the mud and noticed he wore two different-colored socks. His best friend wasn't at school that day. That meant they couldn't share his dessert at lunch. He always counted on that. When he got home, he found out he had to baby-sit his little sister and clean up the mess his puppy made in the kitchen. Dinner was a big disappointment, too. His dad hadn't made any potatoes. Luis loved potatoes. His favorite television show was canceled because of a news bulletin, and his homework took twice as long as usual. For once in his life Luis was looking forward to bedtime.

Answer the questions.

1. Why do you think Luis was looking forward to going to bed?

_____

_____

2. Name three things that happened to Luis to make his day terrible.

_____

_____

3. What might have caused Luis to wake up late for school?

_____

_____

4. Why do you think Luis's best friend wasn't at school? _____

_____

_____

5. What do you think will happen to Luis tomorrow? _____

_____

_____

_____

Earthquakes

Earthquakes are scary natural disasters. During an earthquake, the ground shakes and the earth cracks open. Buildings and bridges collapse. Streets break apart. Fires often occur right after an earthquake because gas pipes break. Sometimes floods happen from broken water pipes.

There are about eighteen big earthquakes every year. It is hard to predict where or when an earthquake will occur. Earthquakes come in groups. An earthquake may begin with foreshocks, or small tremors, at the beginning of the quake. Then there is a main shock, which is the strongest part of the quake. Aftershocks come next. These are smaller quakes that happen as the rocks settle down. Sometimes there are several aftershocks.

Answer the questions.

1. Write one word to tell what this story is about.

_____

2. Write a new title for this story. It must be at least two words.

_____

3. Draw a line under the main idea in the story.

4. List two details that support the main idea.

1._____

2._____

Draw a line to complete each sentence.

Earthquakes are   gas pipes break.

Fires occur because   from broken water pipes.

Floods happen   with foreshocks.

The main shock   are smaller quakes.

Aftershocks   scary natural disasters.

An earthquake might begin   is the strongest part of the quake.

Peteca

"Peteca" is a popular party game in Brazil, a country in South America. You can play by yourself or with several friends. You need a small beanbag or sock filled with sand or salt, three feathers for decoration, and string. First, use the string to tie the feathers to the top of the beanbag or sock. Next, take turns tossing the beanbag up and hitting it with one hand back into the air as many times as you can without letting it touch the ground. With each hit, the player says a letter of the alphabet or begins counting. You can change this part of the game by having the players name a country, count by 10s, or anything else. The player to make it through the most letters or numbers, etc., without dropping or missing the bag wins.

44

Number the steps to play "Peteca" in order from 1 to 5.

_____ Let somebody else have a turn after you drop the beanbag on the ground.

_____ Make a beanbag or sock filled with sand or salt.

_____ Decorate the beanbag with feathers.

_____ Say a letter or count while you are hitting the beanbag into the air.

_____ Take turns tossing the bag up and hitting it with one hand.

Instead of saying the alphabet, counting, or naming countries, what else could you say during the game?

_____

_____

_____

_____

Ben's Leprechaun

Ben found a leprechaun in the park and was granted one wish. He thought about asking that everything he touched turn to gold, but then he remembered how that didn't work out for King Midas. He thought about asking for all the money in the world, but then he remembered reading a story about that. It didn't turn out too well either. He thought about asking for a million dollars, but then he thought, "Is that enough? Who would I give money to? Who wouldn't I give money to? How will I know people like me for myself and not for my money?" After carefully thinking about the situation, he decided to just settle for a hot fudge sundae. That would be the end of the story except that Ben dripped chocolate on his new shirt. The shirt was ruined and his mother grounded him for a week.

Complete the story map, then answer the question.

Main Character
Setting
Plot (important events in the story)

If you met a leprechaun, what would you wish for, and why?

_____

_____

_____

_____

Muffin

Amy found a baby chipmunk near her home. The chipmunk was injured. She carefully placed the chipmunk in a shoe box with tissue paper in the bottom. She had her mother drive her to the veterinarian. The doctor fixed the chipmunk's leg and dressed her cuts.

In a month, the chipmunk Amy called Muffin was as good as new. She had become a part of the family. Amy's dog, Casey, had even gotten used to having Muffin in the house.

One day Amy's father had a talk with her. He explained that chipmunks aren't supposed to be pets. They are wild creatures and should live outside. Amy knew her father was right, but she hated to let Muffin go. She told her father she would think about it.

A few days later, Amy took Muffin back to where she found her and let her go.

Write about what you think might happen next and explain why.

_____

_____

_____

_____

_____

_____

In the space below, draw what you think might happen next.

Cute, but Troublesome

Have you ever heard of sugar gliders? They are **exotic** pets that are about the size of an adult hand. They have soft fur, big round eyes, and can be very loving.

On the other hand, if they become scared, they may run, pinch, bite, or scream. Sugar gliders are **nocturnal**. They can crawl into very small places. In their natural **habitat**, sugar gliders live in groups. Therefore, they need lots of attention, or they could **suffer** from loneliness and might even cause harm to themselves.

A sugar glider likes to climb and has sharp claws and teeth. A sugar glider often mistakes **bare** legs for tree trunks and digs its claws in as it climbs.

Write the letter on the line to match the words from the passage with their meanings.

_____ 1. nocturnal   a. wearing nothing

_____ 2. habitat   b. to undergo something painful

_____ 3. suffer   c. environment

_____ 4. bare   d. active at night

_____ 5. exotic   e. unusual

Write a paragraph persuading a friend why he or she should or should not buy a sugar glider.

_____

_____

_____

_____

_____

_____

_____

Humphrey

Humphrey is the name of a humpback whale that got lost in October of 1985. Although he was as big as a bus and was nearly forty feet long, he was young and inexperienced. He got separated from his pod, or group, and ended up passing underneath the Golden Gate Bridge and into the bay in San Francisco.

Humphrey started following a submarine that he thought might be another whale. That got him into even more trouble. Eventually he ended up swimming into freshwater and was in an area so shallow his flippers were brushing the bottom. He was seventy miles away from the ocean.

Scientists and other concerned people came to help. After several failed attempts, they found something that worked. They got a recording of humpback whales and played if from the back of a boat. Humphrey was led back out to sea where he rejoined his pod.

Use the information in the passage to complete the crossword puzzle.

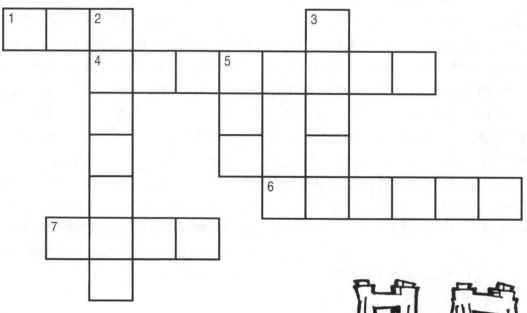

Across
1. Humphrey was as big as a _____.
4. What kind of whale was Humphrey?
6. Golden Gate _____
7. Scientists used a recording of whale sounds to get Humphrey to follow a _____ out to sea.

Down
2. Humphrey's flippers brushed the bottom because the water was _____.
3. Humphrey swam into fresh_____.
5. What is the name of a group of whales?

Fiola's New Game

Fiola and her best friend, Tasha, love to play games. One day Fiola asked, "Why don't we make up a new game?" They decided to draw a square on the sidewalk using chalk so it would be easy to wash off when they were done. They marked off smaller squares inside the large square. Each smaller square had a number that represented the score you could earn if you landed on that space. They tried tossing different things into the square. Fiola tried a sponge but it was so light, it wasn't easy to control. Tasha tried a marble but it just kept rolling out of the square. They finally settled on pebbles from the driveway. Tossing the pebble too high made the pebble bounce too much. Tossing the pebbles too low kept the pebble from bouncing at all. They finally figured out the right technique and started to play the game.

Circle the letter beside each correct answer.

1. The girls decided to draw the square in chalk because it:
   a. would easily wash off.
   b. would be easy to see.
   c. was the only material they had.

2. Fiola decided not to use a sponge because:
   a. it was too big.
   b. it was too small.
   c. it was too light.

3. Tasha decided not to use a marble because:
   a. it was too heavy.
   b. it rolled away.
   c. it was too light.

4. The girls discovered that tossing a pebble too high was a problem because:
   a. it bounced too much when it landed.
   b. the girls couldn't find where it landed.
   c. it didn't bounce enough.

Answer the following questions.

5. What happens if the girls toss the pebble too low? _____

_____

6. How would you play this game? _____

_____

Camping Trip

Thomas and his parents went on a camping trip. They found the perfect spot beside a creek. Thomas and his dad set up the tent while his mom got out the supplies for dinner. When camp was set up, Thomas told his parents that he wanted to go exploring in the creek while the sun was still up. His father told him not to go too far from their campsite and to be careful.

Thomas rolled up his pant legs and waded into the water. He used a stick to poke a few leaves and rocks on the creek bed. Pretty soon he saw something that looked back at him. It was a snake. Thomas jumped out of the water and raced down the dirt path back to camp. Thomas jumped into the car and closed the door.

Answer the questions.

1. What did Thomas and his family do first when they arrived at the campsite?

_____

_____

2. What did Thomas do after that? _____

_____

3. What did Thomas do last? _____

_____

4. What do you think Thomas did next? Finish the story.

_____

_____

_____

_____

_____

_____

Embarrassing Moment

Brenda was a **stubborn** little girl. She wanted to win a swim **meet** and a medal, but she wasn't willing to **train** for it. The local swimming pool offered free lessons and she could have joined the swim team, but she decided she was already good enough.

The first **competition** was **announced** and Brenda signed up. As she watched the races, she noticed that the swimmers started with a racing dive. She had never tried one of those.

Finally, it was her turn. She lined up on the starting block along with the other swimmers. The starting gun was fired and she held her nose and jumped in the water. It felt like an **eternity** before she surfaced. She wiped her eyes and saw that the rest of the swimmers had almost finished the race. She came in last place.

Her father wrapped her in a towel and held her close while she **sobbed**. She was really **embarrassed**.

Write the words from the bubbles next to the correct meanings of the words as they are used in the story.

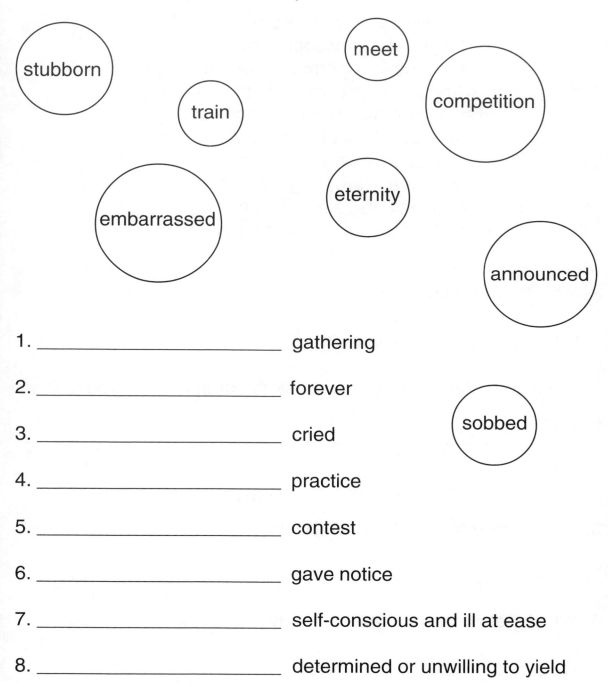

stubborn

meet

train

competition

embarrassed

eternity

announced

1. _____ gathering

2. _____ forever

3. _____ cried

sobbed

4. _____ practice

5. _____ contest

6. _____ gave notice

7. _____ self-conscious and ill at ease

8. _____ determined or unwilling to yield

Pet Problems

I really, really want a pet.
I'll get one very soon, I bet.
My mom says I must think it through
And know just what I want to do.
Bring home a furry, bouncy puppy?
A fishbowl full of swimming guppies?
Shall I choose a purring cat?
Maybe a lizard, frog, or rat?
I haven't made my choice just yet,
But I really, really want a pet.

Answer the questions.

1. What does the author want? _____

2. What does the author's mom think the author should do? Why?

   _____

   _____

3. Name three pets listed in the poem. _____

   _____

4. Which pet would you choose? Why? _____

   _____

   _____